The Beat
Quiz Book

250 Questions To Test Your Knowledge
Of This Incredibly Successful Group

Published by Glowworm Press
7 Nuffield Way
Abingdon OX14 1RL
By Colin Carter

The Beatles Quiz

This book contains two hundred and fifty informative and entertaining trivia questions with multiple choice answers. With 250 questions, some easy, some more demanding, this entertaining book will really test your knowledge of The Beatles.

You will be quizzed on a wide range of topics associated with The Beatles for you to test yourself; with questions on the early days, the songs, the lyrics, the incredible achievements, the awards and much more, guaranteeing you a fun and truly educational experience. The Beatles Quiz Book will provide entertainment for fans of all ages, and will certainly test your knowledge of this world famous group. The book is packed with information and is a must-have for all true Beatles fans, wherever you live in the world.

FOREWORD

When I was asked to write a foreword to this book I was incredibly flattered.

I have known Colin for a number of years and his knowledge of facts and figures is phenomenal.

His love for music and his talent for writing quiz books makes him the ideal man to pay homage to the geniuses that are John, Paul, George and Ringo - The Beatles – the most successful band of all time.

This book came about as a result of a challenge during a round of golf!

I do hope you enjoy the book.

Paul Hoskmeister

OK, let's start with some easy questions.

Chapter 1: Easy Start

1. Which city were all of The Beatles born in?
    A. Leeds
    B. Leicester
    C. Liverpool
    D. London

2. Who was the youngest?
    A. John
    B. Paul
    C. George
    D. Ringo

3. Who was the shortest in height?
    A. John
    B. Paul
    C. George
    D. Ringo

4. When did John and Paul meet for the first time?
    A. January 6th 1957
    B. April 6th 1957
    C. July 6th 1957
    D. October 6th 1957

5. Where did John and Paul meet for the first time?
    A. At a Church fete
    B. At the circus
    C. At a funfair
    D. At school

6. Where did Paul and George meet?
    A. At a snooker club
    B. At school music classes
    C. On a bus
    D. On the River Mersey ferry

7. Which band had John formed before he had met any of the other Beatles?
    A. The Cavemen
    B. The Highwaymen
    C. The Quarrymen
    D. The Weathermen

8. What was the group's early nickname?
    A. The Fab Four
    B. The Fantastic Four
    C. The Fresh Four
    D. The Friendly Four

9. What was the group's first single?
    A. From Me To You
    B. Love Me Do
    C. Please Please Me
    D. She Loves You

10. What was the group's debut album?
    A. Introducing... The Beatles
    B. Meet The Beatles
    C. Please Please Me
    D. With The Beatles

Chapter 1: Answers

A1. All four members of the group were born in Liverpool.

A2. George was the youngest. The order by oldest to youngest was Ringo, John, Paul and George.

A3. Ringo, at 5 feet 6 inches, was the shortest. George was 5 feet 10 inches, John was 5 feet 11 inches and Paul is 5 feet 11 inches tall.

A4. John and Paul met for the first time on July 6th 1957.

A5. John was performing with The Quarrymen at the Woolton Parish Church, Liverpool Garden Fete. After the show Paul introduced himself to John and played him a few songs, including Eddie Cochran's 'Twenty Flight Rock' which obviously impressed him, as two weeks later Paul was asked to join the band.

A6. Paul met George for the first time on a bus on the way to school.

A7. The Quarrymen were formed by John in 1956, which evolved into The Beatles by 1960. The band was named after John's school – Quarry Bank High School.

A8. The band picked up the nickname 'The Fab Four' early in their careers.

A9. 'Love Me Do' was the group's debut single, released in October 1962.

A10. 'Please Please Me' was the first album released by The Beatles, being released in March 1963.

Chapter 2: The Early Days

11. What was the name of the club the band regularly played gigs at in Liverpool?
    A. The Caramel Club
    B. The Casino Club
    C. The Casual Club
    D. The Cavern Club

12. Where did the band play in residence in Germany in the 1960s?
    A. Berlin
    B. Frankfurt
    C. Hamburg
    D. Munich

13. Who was the band's record producer?
    A. Eddie Kramer
    B. George Martin
    C. Tom Parker
    D. Alan Parsons

14. What was Brian Epstein's relationship with the band?
    A. Legal Counsel
    B. Manager
    C. Media Liaison Officer
    D. Physiotherapist

15. Who was the band's road manager?
    A. Mal Elliott
    B. Mal Elliss
    C. Mal Emery
    D. Mal Evans

16. What was the name of the musical movement in Liverpool in the early 1960s?
    A. Mersey Beat
    B. Mersey Mods
    C. Mersey Music
    D. Mersey Tunes

17. Who was the original bass guitarist who left the band in 1961?
    A. Frank Allen
    B. Rory Storm
    C. Stuart Sutcliffe
    D. Terry Sylvester

18. Which record company first signed the Beatles?
    A. Atlantic
    B. Capitol
    C. EMI
    D. Island

19. What is the first track on the 'Please Please Me' album?
    A. I Saw Her Standing There
    B. Love Me Do
    C. Please Please Me
    D. There's a Place

20. What did George Martin say to the group at the end of the studio recording session of 'Please Please Me' in November 1962?
    A. Let's all go and have a pint
    B. Stick with me, and you'll go far
    C. You guys are improving
    D. You've just made your first number one

A11. The Cavern Club was the club the band regularly played gigs at in the early days. The club is still there and regularly has Beatles cover bands playing sets there.

A12. The band played five residencies in total in Hamburg.

A13. The Beatles successfully auditioned for George Martin in June 1962. He was key to The Beatles success and when he died Paul said, "If anyone earned the title of the fifth Beatle, it was George."

A14. Epstein was the group's manager from 1962 until his death in 1967, aged just 32.

A15. Mal Evans was the group's road manager from 1963 to 1970.

A16. Mersey Beat or Merseybeat was the movement that attracted many Liverpool based singers and groups in the early 1960s.

A17. Stuart Sutcliffe was the original bass guitarist in the band. He left to further his career as a painter, yet died in 1962 aged just 21 from a brain haemorrhage. Sutcliffe and John came up with the name "Beetles", as they were both fans of Buddy Holly and the Crickets.

A18. In 1962, George Martin signed the band to EMI's Parlophone label.

A19. The first track on the 'Please Please Me' album is 'I Saw Her Standing There' a song primarily written by Paul.

A20. After encouraging the group to re-record 'Please Please Me' at a faster tempo, Martin declared to the group, "You've just made your first Number One."

21. What was his middle name?
    A. Washington
    B. Watson
    C. Wellington
    D. Winston

22. What instrument did he play in the band?
    A. Bass Guitar
    B. Drums
    C. Lead Guitar
    D. Rhythm Guitar

23. Which of these brand of Gibson guitars is he most closely associated with?
    A. Les Paul Classic
    B. Les Paul Junior
    C. Les Paul Senior
    D. Les Paul Standard

24. Who told him, "The guitar's all very well, but you'll never make a living at it"?
    A. His Aunt
    B. His Father
    C. His Headmaster
    D. His Uncle

25. What was his first book called?
    A. A Hard Days Write
    B. Don't Write Me Off
    C. In His Own Write
    D. Never Write, Never Wrong

26. What nationality was his second wife Yoko Ono?
    A. Chinese
    B. Japanese
    C. Korean
    D. Malaysian

27. How many children did John have?
    A. 1
    B. 2
    C. 3
    D. 4

28. What was the first song he ever wrote?
    A. Free As a Bird
    B. Hello Little Girl
    C. Love of the Loved
    D. Till There Was You

29. What was the name of the black comedy he filmed in 1967?
    A. Dogs of War
    B. How I Won The War
    C. Oh! What A Lovely War
    D. The War Of The Roses

30. How old was he when he died?
    A. 40
    B. 42
    C. 44
    D. 46

A21. John's middle name was Winston, named in honour of Winston Churchill.

A22. John mainly played rhythm guitar in the band.

A23. A Les Paul Junior is the guitar most closely associated with John.

A24. That quote is attributed to his Aunt and parental guardian, Mimi Smith.

A25. 'In His Own Write' was John's first book, first published n March 1964. It mainly consists of short stories and poems.

A26. Yoko Ono was born in Japan.

A27. John has two sons – Julian and Sean.

A28. 'Hello Little Girl' was the first song John wrote. He wrote it back in 1957 and in 1963 a Merseybeat band called The Fourmost recorded it and the song reached number nine in the UK charts. It is worth tracking it down on YouTube.

A29. 'How I Won The War' is the name of the movie, and it was his only appearance in a non-Beatles feature film. A photo of John playing his character of Musketeer Gripweed made it to the cover of the very first issue of Rolling Stone magazine.

A30. He died tragically aged just 40, shot outside his apartment in New York City.

31. What instrument did he play in the band?
    A. Bass Guitar
    B. Drums
    C. Lead Guitar
    D. Rhythm Guitar

32. What was he known as?
    A. The bossy Beatle
    B. The clever Beatle
    C. The cute Beatle
    D. The sweet Beatle

33. What was the first song Paul ever wrote?
    A. I Lost My Little Brother
    B. I Lost My Little Darling
    C. I Lost My Little Girl
    D. I Lost My Little Heart

34. What was his first wife's original name?
    A. Jane Asher
    B. Linda Eastman
    C. Heather Mills
    D. Nancy Shevell

35. How many children does Paul have?
    A. 2
    B. 3
    C. 4
    D. 5

36. Which of these songs did he play piano on?
    A. A Day in the Life
    B. Hey Jude
    C. Lady Madonna
    D. The Long and Winding Road

37. Who made the 500/1 violin bass guitar he played in the early years of The Beatles?
    A. Fender
    B. Gresch
    C. Hofner
    D. Wal

38. What story created a media frenzy in 1969?
    A. Paul came out as gay
    B. Paul had died two years before and had been replaced by an imposter
    C. Paul had undergone a sex change
    D. Paul's long lost twin brother was discovered

39. What was the name of the band he formed in 1971?
    A. Lapwings
    B. Waxwings
    C. Wings
    D. Wingspan

40. When did Paul receive a knighthood?
    A. 1993
    B. 1995
    C. 1997
    D. 1999

A31. Paul was the band's bass guitarist.

A32. He was knowns as the cute Beatle.

A33. 'I Lost My little Girl' is widely acknowledged as the first song Paul ever wrote – at the age of 14.

A34. Paul married his first wife Linda Eastman in March 1969.

A35. Paul has five children in total, one son and four daughters.

A36. Paul played piano on all of these songs. Give yourself a bonus point if you knew that. He was a very accomplished pianist.

A37. Paul mainly used a Hofner 500/1 bass during the early years of the band.

A38. The bizarre rumour was that Paul had died in a car crash and had been replaced in the band by someone else. Needless to say, it wasn't true.

A39. Paul formed the band Wings in 1971. The name came to him when he was praying for the successful birth of his daughter Stella and an image of wings came to his mind.

A40. Sir Paul McCartney was knighted for his services to music in 1997.

41. What was he known as?
    A. The hairy Beatle
    B. The noisy Beatle
    C. The posh Beatle
    D. The quiet Beatle

42. What instrument did he play in the band?
    A. Bass Guitar
    B. Drums
    C. Lead Guitar
    D. Rhythm Guitar

43. Which of these songs did he write?
    A. Here Come the Sun
    B. Something
    C. Taxman
    D. While My Guitar Gently Weeps

44. Which band did he form before he had met any of the other Beatles?
    A. The Extremists
    B. The Mutineers
    C. The Pirates
    D. The Rebels

45. Which brand of guitar is he most closely associated with?
    A. Fender
    B. Gibson
    C. Gretsch
    D. Rickenbacker

46. What spirituality did he incorporate into some Beatles' material?
    A. Buddhism
    B. Hinduism
    C. Islam
    D. Sikhism

47. Who taught George how to play sitar?
    A. Nikhil Banerjee
    B. Chaganti Koteswara
    C. Ravi Shankar
    D. Sachin Tendulkar

48. What is his most successful solo single?
    A. All Those Years Ago
    B. Give Me Love (Give Me Peace on Earth)
    C. Got My Mind Set On You
    D. My Sweet Lord

49. What was the name of the band he formed in 1988 that included Bob Dylan, Jeff Lynne and Tom Petty?
    A. Traveling Danburys
    B. Traveling Gooseberrys
    C. Traveling Mulberrys
    D. Traveling Wilburys

50. How old was he when he died?
    A. 56
    B. 57
    C. 58
    D. 59

A41. George was known as the quiet Beatle.

A42. George was the band's lead guitarist.

A43. George composed all of these songs. Give yourself a bonus point if you knew that.

A44. George formed The Rebels when he was just 16 years old with his brother and a friend.

A45. George played many brands of guitar in his life but he is mostly closely associated with a Fender Stratocaster.

A46. George embraced Indian culture and Hinduism spirituality.

A47. Ravi Shankar taught George how to play the sitar.

A48. 'My Sweet Lord' is George's most successful solo single. It was recorded at Abbey Road Studios

A49. He formed the platinum-selling supergroup Traveling Wilburys in 1988.

A50. He died aged just 58, from lung cancer.

Chapter 6: Ringo Starr

51. What is Ringo's real name?
    A. Richard Sharkey
    B. Richard Snarkey
    C. Richard Sparkey
    D. Richard Starkey

52. What instrument did he play in the band?
    A. Bass Guitar
    B. Drums
    C. Lead Guitar
    D. Rhythm Guitar

53. Which band was he a member of before he joined The Beatles?
    A. Cory Storm and the Cyclones
    B. Dory Storm and the Tornados
    C. Rory Storm and the Hurricanes
    D. Tory Storm and the Typhoons

54. Which of these songs did he sing lead vocals on?
    A. I am the Walrus
    B. Here Comes The Sun
    C. The Fool on the Hill
    D. Yellow Submarine

55. Which of these songs did he write?
    A. Golden Slumbers
    B. Maxwell's Silver Hammer
    C. Mean Mr Mustard
    D. Octopus's Garden

56. How did he get the name Ringo?
    A. His ringing drumming style
    B. He used to fit door bells for a living
    C. He wore many rings
    D. He used to be a postman

57. Which famous actress did he marry in 1981?
    A. Barbara Bach
    B. Barbara Eden
    C. Barbara Hershey
    D. Barbara Windsor

58. Which brand of drums did Ringo play in his heyday?
    A. Gretsch
    B. Ludwig
    C. Pearl
    D. Sonor

59. Who did Ringo replace when he joined The Beatles?
    A. Andy Best
    B. George Best
    C. Pete Best
    D. Tom Best

60. Which TV series did he narrate for two series in the 1980s?
    A. Bob the Builder
    B. Little Red Tractor
    C. Postman Pat
    D. Thomas the Tank Engine

Chapter 6: Answers

A51. Ringo was born as Richard Starkey.

A52. This is an easy one. He was of course the band's drummer.

A53. He left Rory Storm and the Hurricanes to join The Beatles.

A54. Ringo sang lead vocal on 'Yellow Submarine'. It is the group's' only number one in the UK with Ringo as lead singer.

A55. Ringo is credited with writing and singing 'Octopus's Garden'. Later in life, he wrote a children's book named after the song.

A56. His name came about because of all the rings he wore on his fingers.

A57. He married former Bond girl Barbara Bach in April 1981. They met on the set of the film 'Caveman' the year before.

A58. Ringo's drum kit for most of his career was a Ludwig Oyster.

A59. Pete Best was the drummer that Ringo replaced.

A60. Ringo narrated 'Thomas the Tank Engine and Friends' to give the show its full title.

Chapter 7

61. How many consecutive nights did the band play at The Top Ten Club in Hamburg in 1961?
    A. 62
    B. 72
    C. 82
    D. 92

62. Who has a statue outside the Cavern Club in Liverpool?
    A. John
    B. Paul
    C. George
    D. Ringo

63. What was the band's second single?
    A. Can't Buy Me Love
    A. From Me To You
    B. Please Please Me
    C. She Loves You

64. What song did Paul write for Badfinger?
    A. Baby Blue
    B. Come and Get It
    C. Day After Day
    D. No Matter What

65. Where did John and Paul write 'From Me To You'?
    A. At a funfair
    B. At school
    C. On a bus
    D. On a plane

66. When did The Beatles play the Cavern Club for the first time?
    A. 1958
    B. 1959
    C. 1960
    D. 1961

67. What did The Beatles do on January 1st 1962?
    A. Audition for Decca
    B. Meet Brian Epstein for the first time
    C. Play the Cavern Club for the final time
    D. Sign their first record contract

68. What was the band's third single?
    A. Ain't She Sweet
    B. Can't Buy Me Love
    C. From Me To You
    D. She Loves You

69. What did George Harrison say he didn't like about George Martin when he first met him?
    A. His accent
    B. His stare
    C. His suit
    D. His tie

70. How long did it take John and Paul to write 'She Loves You'?
    A. Two days
    B. Two weeks
    C. Two months
    D. Two years

A61. The band played a staggering 92 nights in a row at The Top Ten Club in Hamburg in 1961.

A62. There are numerous statues of the Beatles in Liverpool, but it is a statue of John on his own that stands outside The Cavern Club in the city centre.

A63. 'Please Please Me' released in January 1963 in the UK was the group's second single to be released.

A64. 'Come and Get It' was written by Paul. He gave it to Badfinger who had a major hit with the song.

A65. John and Paul wrote 'From Me To You' on a bus while they were touring with Helen Shapiro. The song title was inspired by the letters section of the New Musical Express called "From You to Us."

A66. Thursday 9th February 1961 was the first time The Beatles played at the Cavern Club. Their fee was just £5 – to be shared between the four of them!

A67. They auditioned for Decca Records. Head of A&R at Decca Dick Rowe decided not to sign the group to a record deal telling Epstein, "Guitar groups are on their way out."

A68. 'From Me to You' was the band's third single, released in April 1963, and it made it to number 1 in the UK charts.

A69. When George Martin first met the group, he asked them if there was anything they didn't like. George replied, "I don't like your tie" thus setting the cheeky tone for their relationship from day one.

A70. John and Paul wrote the song after a concert in Newcastle in just two days, and it was recorded less than a week after it was written.

71. Who said, "I hate the idea of success robbing you of your private life"?
    A. John
    B. Paul
    C. George
    D. Ringo

72. Who said, "I'd rather be a musician than a pop star"?
    A. John
    B. Paul
    C. George
    D. Ringo

73. Who said, "I don't believe in killing whatever the reason"?
    A. John
    B. Paul
    C. George
    D. Ringo

74. Who said, "People in Liverpool don't move very far, you know"?
    A. John
    B. Paul
    C. George
    D. Ringo

75. Who said, "I wanted to be successful, not famous"?
    A. John
    B. Paul
    C. George
    D. Ringo

76. Who said, "Count your age by friends, not years"?
    A. John
    B. Paul
    C. George
    D. Ringo

77. Who said, "I don't ever try to make a serious social comment"?
    A. John
    B. Paul
    C. George
    D. Ringo

78. Who said, "America: It's like Britain, only with buttons"?
    A. John
    B. Paul
    C. George
    D. Ringo

79. Who said, "It's better to be an outspoken atheist than a hypocrite"?
    A. John
    B. Paul
    C. George
    D. Ringo

80. Who said, "You can judge a man's true character by the way he treats his fellow animals"?
    A. John
    B. Paul
    C. George
    D. Ringo

Chapter 8: Answers

A71. Paul said, "I hate the idea of success robbing you of your private life"

A72. George said, "I'd rather be a musician than a pop star"

A73. John said, "I don't believe in killing whatever the reason"

A74. Ringo said, "People in Liverpool don't move very far, you know"

A75. George said, "I wanted to be successful, not famous"

A76. John said, "Count your age by friends, not years"

A77. Paul said, "I don't ever try to make a serious social comment"

A78. Ringo said, "America: It's like Britain, only with buttons"

A79. George said, "It's better to be an outspoken atheist than a hypocrite"

A80. Paul said, "You can judge a man's true character by the way he treats his fellow animals"

Chapter 9

81. Who had a major hit in the UK with the Lennon-McCartney composition 'Do You Want To Know A Secret?'
    A. Cliff Bennett and the Rebel Rousers
    B. Billy J. Kramer with the Dakotas
    C. Freddie and the Dreamers
    D. Gerry and the Pacemakers

82. How old was Paul when he wrote 'Yesterday'?
    A. 22
    B. 23
    C. 24
    D. 25

83. Who said, "We're more popular than Jesus now"?
    A. John
    B. Paul
    C. George
    D. Ringo

84. Which song knocked 'She Loves You' off the top of the charts in the UK?
    A. All My Loving
    B. Can't Buy Me Love
    C. I Feel Fine
    D. I Want To Hold Your Hand

85. Who was Peter, of Peter and Gordon fame, who Paul wrote a number of hits for?
    A. Jane Asher's brother
    B. Paul's best friend at school
    C. Ringo's hairdresser
    D. A winner of a talent show competition

86. Which of these features as a stone statue on the cover of the Sergeant Pepper album?
    A. Cinderella
    B. Goldilocks
    C. Sleeping Beauty
    D. Snow White

87. What is the name of the long running Cirque de Soleil Beatles themed show in Las Vegas?
    A. All You Need Is Love
    B. Can't Buy Me Love
    C. LOVE
    D. Love Me Do

88. Where do The Beatles rank in the list of best selling music artists of all time?
    A. 1st
    B. 2nd
    C. 3rd
    D. 4th

89. Which song contains the line "Oh, the judge he guilty found her for robbing a homeward bounder"?
    A. Dizzy Miss Lizzy
    B. Eleanor Rigby
    C. Honey Pie
    D. Maggie Mae

90. When is World Beatles Day?
    A. 25th April
    B. 25th June
    C. 25th August
    D. 25th October

A81. Billy J. Kramer with the Dakotas had a major hit with 'Do You Want To Know A Secret?" in 1963.

A82. Paul completed 'Yesterday' whilst on holiday in Portugal in May 1965 and the record was recorded at Abbey Road Studios on 14th June 1965 four days before Paul's 23rd birthday.

A83. John said, "We're more popular than Jesus now" in an interview with the Evening Standard in March 1966.

A84. The follow up single to 'She Loves You' was 'I Want To Hold Your Hand'. Written by John and Paul together at Jane Asher's parents' house in London, it sold more than a million copies on advanced orders alone.

A85. Peter Asher was Jane's brother. Amongst the songs Paul wrote for Peter and Gordon were 'A World Without Love'; 'Nobody I Know' and 'I Don't Want To See You Again'.

A86. A small statue of Snow White is included on the Sergeant Pepper album cover.

A87. LOVE is the name of the Cirque de Soleil Beatles themed show in Las Vegas. It plays to sell-out crowds every night at The Mirage.

A88. The Beatles are ranked number one best selling band in history, with EMI Records estimating sales of over one billion units.

A89. 'Maggie Mae', which was a traditional Liverpudlian folk song, contains the lyrics, "Oh, the judge he guilty found her for robbing a homeward bounder, That dirty no-good robbin' Maggie Mae."

A90. World Beatles Day, also known as Global Beatles Day, is on 25th June each year. The date commemorates the group performing 'All You Need Is Love' on a BBC programme in 1967.

Chapter 10

91. Which Beatle was the first to get married?
    A. John
    B. Paul
    C. George
    D. Ringo

92. Who wrote 'The Beatles: The Authorised Biography' in 1968?
    A. Hunter Davies
    B. Geoff Emerick
    C. Mark Lewisohn
    D. Barry Miles

93. Which Bond movie did Paul write the theme song to?
    A. For Your Eyes Only
    B. Licence To Kill
    C. Live and Let Die
    D. You Only Live Twice

94. Which song did John and Paul write for The Rolling Stones?
    A. As Tears Go By
    B. I Wanna Be Your Man
    C. Not Fade Away
    D. Paint It Black

95. What is the most covered Beatles song?
    A. Hey Jude
    B. Michelle
    C. Something
    D. Yesterday

96. What was their first single to sell a million copies?
    A. Day Tripper
    B. Hey Jude
    C. I Want To Hold Your Hand
    D. She Loves You

97. What was the name of the corporation set up in 1968 to oversee projects related to the band's legacy?
    A. Apple Core
    B. Apple Corps
    C. Apple Peel
    D. Apple Stalk

98. Who had a major hit with 'Jealous Guy'?
    A. King Crimson
    B. Roxy Music
    C. Spandau Ballet
    D. Ultravox

99. What song contains the lyric "A love like ours, could never die; As long as I have you near me"?
    A. Ain't She Sweet
    B. And I Love Her
    C. Do You Want To Know A Secret?
    D. Eight Days A Week

100. Which song did Siouxsie and The Banshees cover?
    A. Come Together
    B. Dear Prudence
    C. Drive My Car
    D. You've Got To Hide Your Love Away

A91. John was the first Beatle to get married when he wed his first wife Cynthia Powell in August 1962.

A92. Hunter Davies wrote the authorised biography with full co-operation of The Beatles. It details the band's career up until the book's publication in 1968.

A93. Paul wrote the theme song to the 1973 movie 'Live and Let Die'.

A94. John and Paul completed writing 'I Wanna Be Your Man' at a recording studio in Soho, London whilst Mick Jagger and the rest of the Stones looked on. The Beatles later recorded their version of the song with Ringo on lead vocals. Incidentally the Stones' version was the first song performed on the first edition of BBC's Top of the Pops in January 1964.

A95. According to Guinness World Records, 'Yesterday' takes the accolade of the most covered song in history having been recorded by well over 2,000 other artists.

A96. 'She Loves You' was the group's first single to sell a million copies.

A97. Apple Corps was the name of the corporation set up in 1968 to oversee projects related to the band's legacy.

A98. Roxy Music reached number 1 in the UK charts in 1971 with their atmospheric version of 'Jealous Guy'.

A99. "A love like ours, could never die; As long as I have you near me" comes from 'And I Love Her' recorded in 1964.

A100. Siouxsie and the Banshees covered 'Dear Prudence' in 1983, and it reached number 3 in the UK charts.

Chapter 11

101. Who was the 2009 biopic film 'Nowhere Boy' about?
    A. John
    B. Paul
    C. George
    D. Ringo

102. What is their best selling song of all time?
    A. Can't Buy Me Love
    B. I Feel Fine
    C. I Want To Hold Your Hand
    D. She Loves You

103. What has Mike McGear got to do with Paul?
    A. He is Paul's yoga teacher
    B. He is Paul's younger brother
    C. He taught Paul how to play piano
    D. He co-wrote Paul's official autobiography

104. What was the name of the song Elton John wrote for John?
    A. Cry to Heaven
    B. Empty Garden
    C. Funeral for a Friend
    D. Sacrifice

105. Which of these authors is featured on the cover of the Sergeant Pepper album?
    A. Emily Bronte
    B. Lewis Carroll
    C. Charles Dickens
    D. George Orwell

106. Which song starts with the line "Flew in from Miami Beach, BOAC"?
    A. Across The Universe
    B. Back in the USSR
    C. I Am The Walrus
    D. The Fool On The Hill

107. What was the name of The Beatles only ever Christmas themed single?
    A. Christmas Time (Is Here Again)
    B. Happy Xmas (War Is Over)
    C. Winter Wonderland
    D. Wonderful Christmas Time

108. Who is barefoot and out of step with the others on the cover of the Abbey Road album?
    A. John
    B. Paul
    C. George
    D. Ringo

109. How many years ago today since Sergeant Pepper taught the band to play?
    A. Ten
    B. Twenty
    C. Thirty
    D. Forty

110. Which Pirates of the Caribbean movie did Paul play the part of Uncle Jack?
    A. At World's End
    B. Dead Men Tell No Tales
    C. On Stranger Tides
    D. The Curse of the Black Pearl

Chapter 11: Answers

A101. 'Nowhere Boy' is a biographical drama film that concentrates on John's adolescence.

A102. Released in August 1963, 'She Loves You' is the group's best selling song of all time.

A103. Mike is Paul's younger brother.

A104. 'Empty Garden (Hey Hey Johnny)' is a song written as a tribute to John Lennon, who had been assassinated 18 months earlier. The song title 'Empty Garden' refers to the huge pile of flowers left behind by mourners outside The Dakota, Lennon's home in New York City, near the site where he was assassinated.

A105. Lewis Carroll, who wrote Alice's Adventures in Wonderland, is featured on the Sergeant Pepper album cover.

A106. This is the first line to 'Back in the USSR'. The USSR stood for the Union of Soviet Socialist Republics – the Soviet Union, including Russia; and BOAC was the forerunner to British Airways.

A107. 'Christmas Time (Is Here Again)' was the only Christmas themed song the band released as a single. It was officially released in 1995 on the 'Free as a Bird' single. As an aside, the band created special Christmas mini-albums each year from 1963 to 1969 which were sent by post to members of the official fan club.

A108. Paul is the one out of step with the others, and he is also not wearing any socks or shoes.

A109. The opening lyrics to 'Sergeant Pepper's Lonely Hearts Club Band' are, "It was twenty years ago today that Sergeant Pepper taught the band to play."

A110. Paul played the part of Uncle Jack in 'Pirates of the Caribbean: Dead Men Tell No Tales'.

111. How many studio albums did the group make?
    A. 11
    B. 12
    C. 13
    D. 14

112. When was the first time the word Beatlemania was used by a newspaper?
    A. September 1963
    B. October 1963
    C. November 1963
    D. December 1963

113. Who went on to become a successful movie producer?
    A. John
    B. Paul
    C. George
    D. Ringo

114. Which song contains the lyric "If there's anything that you want, if there's anything I can do"?
    A. Ain't She Sweet
    B. And I Love Her
    C. Do You Want To Know A Secret?
    D. From Me To You

115. Who has a daughter who is a well known fashion designer?
    A. John
    B. Paul
    C. George
    D. Ringo

116. Who was the inspiration for 'Dear Prudence'?
   A. Prudence Courteney
   B. Prudence Farrow
   C. Prue Leith
   D. Prudence McIntyre

117. Who did the group refer to as Mr. Fixit?
   A. Geoff Emerick
   B. Mal Evans
   C. Norman Smith
   D. Alistair Taylor

118. Who was Paul trying to sound like when the group recorded 'Long Tall Sally'?
   A. Chuck Berry
   B. Bo Diddley
   C. Jerry Lee Lewis
   D. Little Richard

119. Which member of The Rolling Stones sang backing vocals on 'Yellow Submarine'?
   A. Mick Jagger
   B. Brian Jones
   C. Keith Richards
   D. Bill Wyman

120. Who played piano on the single 'Revolution'?
   A. Keith Emerson
   B. Nicky Hopkins
   C. Elton John
   D. Rick Wakeman

Chapter 12: Answers

A111. The group produced a total of 13 studio albums and one compilation album.

A112. There is a dispute on this. The Daily Mirror is credited with using the phrase Beatlemania for the first time in November 1963, after a concert in Cheltenham of all places, and the newspaper headline is easily found by searching online. Some say the word Beatlemania first appeared in a feature in The Daily Mail in October 1963 but we have been unable to verify this.

A113. George Harrison went on to forge a career as a movie producer, making many movies including Time Bandits, Mona Lisa, Shanghai Surprise and Withnail and I.

A114. "If there's anything that you want, if there's anything I can do, just call on me and I'll send it along with love from me to you" is the opening verse to 'From Me To You'.

A115. Paul's daughter Stella is a very successful high-end fashion designer.

A116. Prudence Farrow, sister of actress Mia Farrow, was the inspiration for 'Dear Prudence'. John and George tried to coax her out of her isolation during her obsessive meditation during their time together in India, which led to John writing the song.

A117. Alistair Taylor was referred to as Mr. Fixit by the group due to his ability to find solutions to their requests. Taylor was Epstein's personal assistant and was with Epstein when they saw the group play for the first time at the Cavern Club on 9t November 1961 and he also served as a witness to the group's first contract with Epstein.

A118. Paul tried to sound like Little Richard, who he admired greatly and who originally recorded 'Long Tall Sally'.

A119 Brian Jones, the lead guitarist for The Rolling Stones at the time, sang backing vocals on 'Yellow Submarine'.

A120 Nicky Hopkins played electric piano on the 'Revolution' single. He was a hugely talented pianist who recorded with many groups including The Kinks, The Who and The Rolling Stones.

Chapter 13

121. What were the last words spoken in 'Strawberry Fields Forever'?
    A. Cranberry Sauce
    B. I Buried Paul
    C. Living Is Easy With Eyes Closed
    D. Nothing is Real and Nothing To Get Hung About

122. Who were the first group signed by the Beatles Apple label?
    A. The Climbers
    B. The Creepers
    C. The Iveys
    D. The Vines

123. What is the longest song the Beatles ever recorded?
    A. A Day in the Life
    B. Hey Jude
    C. I Want You (She's So Heavy)
    D. Revolution Number 9

124. How many UK number one albums did the group have?
    A. 12
    B. 13
    C. 14
    D. 15

125. What did some of the audience throw onto stage in Sydney during the band's 1964 tour of Australia?
    A. Gummy Bears
    B. Jelly Babies
    C. Pairs of Knickers
    D. Wine Gums

126. What instrument did George play on 'Strawberry Fields Forever'?
    A. Sarangi
    B. Sitar
    C. Swarmandal
    D. Tambura

127. Who contributed the line "Sea of blue and sky of green" to 'Yellow Submarine'?
    A. Donovan
    B. Ralph McTell
    C. Cat Stevens
    D. Al Stewart

128. How many times did The Beatles play the Cavern Club in total?
    A. 220
    B. 240
    C. 260
    D. 280

129. What is the shortest song, at just 23 seconds long, the group ever recorded?
    A. Golden Slumbers
    B. Her Majesty
    C. Mean Mr Mustard
    D. Polythene Pam

130. What was the German language version of 'She Loves You' called?
    A. Das ist mir wurst
    B. Druck mir die daumen
    C. Fix und fertig sein
    D. Sie Liebt Dich

Chapter 13: Answers

A121. A common belief is that John says, "I Buried Paul" at the end of 'Strawberry Fields Forever' on the Magical Mystery Tour album. He actually says, "Cranberry Sauce", not once, but twice.

A122. The Iveys were the first group signed by the Apple label. They however quickly renamed themselves to Badfinger and recorded five albums for Apple, and went on to sell approximately 14 million albums.

A123. The longest "song" the group recorded is 'Revolution 9' at 8 minutes and 22 seconds long. If you don't regards that as a song, then 'I Want You (She's So Heavy)' takes the accolade at 7minutes and 49 seconds.

A124. The group had fifteen number one albums on the UK charts.

A125. After George had said earlier in the year that he liked jelly babies, fans took it upon themselves to throw packs onto the stage in Sydney. So many were thrown, the band had to stop the show twice.

A126. George played swarmandal on 'Strawberry Fields Forever'. The instrument is also known as an Indian harp.

A127. Scottish singer Donovan contributed the line "Sea of blue and sky of green" to the song when Paul visited his flat in London and told him he needed help with one line.

A128. Beatles historians generally agree that the group played a minimum of 155 lunchtime and 125 evening shows; so 280 in total, until their final performance on 3rd August 1963.

A129. 'Her Majesty' appears on the Abbey Road album. It is just 23 seconds long.

A130. 'Sie liebt dich' was recorded along with 'Komm, gib mir deine hand' (I want to hold your hand) in January 1964. It is the only time in their history that the group recorded a special foreign language version of any of their songs.

131. Which airline did The Beatles fly to America with on their
    first visit?
    A. BOAC
    B. Continental
    C. Pan Am
    D. TWA

132. What was their first TV performance in the US?
    A. Hullabaloo
    B. Shindig
    C. The Ed Sullivan Show
    D. The Grand Ole Opry

133. Where did The Beatles play their first US gig?
    A. Dallas
    B. Los Angeles
    C. New York City
    D. Washington DC

134. How many people attended the concert at Shea Stadium
    in New York in 1965?
    A. 25,300
    B. 35,400
    C. 45,500
    D. 55,600

135. Who was the promoter for the Shea Stadium concert?
    A. Sid Bernstein
    B. Harvey Goldsmith
    C. Bill Graham
    D. Barry Hearn

136. What was the first Lennon-McCartney tune to enter the US charts?
    A. From Me To You
    B. Love Me Do
    C. Please Please Me
    D. She Loves You

137. When did the group occupy all top 5 positions on the Billboard Hot 100?
    A. February 1964
    B. April 1964
    C. June 1964
    D. August 1964

138. What was the only million selling Beatles single in the US that was a cover song?
    A. A Taste of Honey
    B. Rock and Roll Music
    C. Roll Over Beethoven
    D. Twist and Shout

139. How many US number one singles did the group have?
    A. 14
    B. 16
    C. 18
    D. 20

140. Where did The Beatles play their final concert before a paying audience?
    A. Candlestick Park
    B. Dodgers Stadium
    C. Fenway Park
    D. Wrigley Field

Chapter 14: Answers

A131. On 7th February 1964, The Beatles arrived at Kennedy International Airport, New York City from London having travelled on Pan American World Airways Flight 101. They were welcomed by an estimated 4,000 fans and 200 journalists.

A132. The group gave their first live US television performance on The Ed Sullivan Show in February 1964. It was watched by an estimated 73 million people.

A133. The group played their fist live gig in the US at the Washington Coliseum on 11th February 1964.

A134. 55,600 people attended the concert at Shea Stadium in August 1965, the most that have ever attended a rock concert. What might seem commonplace today was a complete first at the time.

A135. Sid Bernstein was the promoter who booked The Beatles for Shea Stadium. He was an important promoter during the so-called British invasion in the 1960s having business relationships with The Kinks, Herman's Hermits and The Rolling Stones among others.

A136. Del Shannon performed on the same bill as The Beatles at the Albert Hall, London in May 1963. He asked John and Paul if he could record one of their songs in the US. They said yes and he recorded 'From Me To You' which charted in the US in June 1963, becoming the first Lennon-McCartney composition in the US charts.

A137. For the week of 4th April 1964, in an achievement that is extremely unlikely ever to be equalled, The Beatles occupied all of the top five positions of the Billboard Hot 100 chart.

A138. 'Twist and Shout' was the only million selling Beatles single in the US that was a cover song.

A139. The group had twenty number one singles on the US Billboard charts.

A140. On 29th August 1966 the group played their final concert before a paying audience at Candlestick Park in San Francisco.

Chapter 15

141. Which song did, "JoJo left his home in Tucson, Arizona for some California grass"?
    A. All Together Now
    B. Get Back
    C. Got To Get You Into My Life
    D. The Long and Winding Road

142. Who said, "these Beatles are very un-American and they take drugs."
    A. Billy Graham
    B. Richard Nixon
    C. Elvis Presley
    D. Frank Sinatra

143. Which of these Chuck Berry songs did the Beatles record?
    A. Johnny B. Goode
    B. Rock and Roll Music
    C. Roll Over Beethoven
    D. Sweet Little Sixteen

144. How many Chuck Berry songs did the Beatles record in total?
    A. 3
    B. 5
    C. 7
    D. 9

145. What was their first song to feature just acoustic instruments?
    A. Ain't She Sweet
    B. And I Love Her
    C. Do You Want To Know A Secret?
    D. Eight Days A Week

146. What was the name of the parody group created by Eric Idle?
    A. The Bootles
    B. The Chuckles
    C. The Fretles
    D. The Rutles

147. Which of these is a popular Beatles tribute act?
    A. The Bootleg Beatles
    B. The Fab Four
    C. The Ultimate Beatles
    D. The Undercover Beatles

148. What did George say after the last Beatles concert?
    A. Beatlemania has bitten the dust
    B. Thank you for the music
    C. Thanks for all your support
    D. That's it. I'm not a Beatle anymore

149. Where was 'Can't Buy Me Love' recorded?
    A. London
    B. New York
    C. Paris
    D. Tokyo

150. What instrument did Ringo play on 'P.S. I Love You'?
    A. Bongo
    B. Harmonica
    C. Maraca
    D. Recorder

A141. "JoJo left his home in Tucson, Arizona for some California grass" is from 'Get Back'.

A142. Elvis Presley said this to then President Richard Nixon. It was an ironic statement considering all the drug issues Elvis had in his life.

A143. Proving what a huge influence Chuck Berry was, all four of these songs were recorded by The Beatles.

A144. The Beatles recorded nine Chuck Berry songs in total. This is far more than any other artist they covered.

A145. 'And I Love Her' was the first Beatles track to feature just acoustic instruments (Ringo played bongos).

A146. The Rutles were created by Eric Idle, of Monty Python fame. They performed visual and aural parodies of the group's songs on a TV comedy show called Rutland Weekend Television in the mid 1970s. Their song titles included 'A Hard Day's Rut', 'All You Need is Cash' and 'Not Letting It Be'.

A147. All four are Beatles tribute acts, but perhaps the most popular is The Bootleg Beatles who have performed over 4,000 shows since they were established in 1980.

A148. After all the equipment had been packed away at Candlestick Park, George said, "That's it. I'm not a Beatle anymore."

A149. 'Can't Buy Me Love' was written and recorded in Paris. Whist the band were doing 18 concerts in Paris in January 1964, they stayed at the George V Hotel, and an upright piano was moved into one of their suites so song writing could continue.

A150. The single 'P.S. I Love You' was recorded with session drummer Andy White. Ringo played supporting maracas.

Chapter 16

151. Who speaks words of wisdom in 'Let It Be'?
    A. Jesus Christ
    B. Mother Mary
    C. My Saviour
    D. The Holy Ghost

152. What did John and Paul call themselves when they played as a duo?
    A. The Berk Twins
    B. The Jerk Twins
    C. The Merk Twins
    D. The Nerk Twins

153. What distinctive sound starts 'I Feel Fine'?
    A. 12 string guitar
    B. Feedback
    C. Tambourine
    D. Trumpet

154. Where did the phrase 'Eight Days a Week' originate?
    A. Paul's brother
    B. Paul's chauffeur
    C. Paul's hairdresser
    D. Paul's tailor

155. Which of these songs did Earth, Wind and Fire cover?
    A. Come Together
    B. Do You Want To Know A Secret
    C. Got to Get You Into My Life
    D. We Can Work It Out

156. What is Lovely Rita's job?
    A. Barmaid
    B. Librarian
    C. Nurse
    D. Meter Maid

157. What song starts with "Here I stand head in hand, turn my face to the wall"?
    A. Do You Want To Know A Secret?
    B. I Saw Her Standing There
    C. Misery
    D. You've Got To Hide Your Love Away

158. What was the name of the band John started in 1969?
    A. The Metal Ono Band
    B. The Plastic Ono Band
    C. The Rubber Ono Band
    D. The Wobbly Ono Band

159. In 1974 Elton John released his cover version of which song?
    A. Back in the USSR
    B. Eleanor Rigby
    C. Lucy in the Sky with Diamonds
    D. Twist and Shout

160. Which film was 'Ticket To Ride' featured in?
    A. A Hard Days Night
    B. Help!
    C. Magical Mystery Tour
    D. Yellow Submarine

A151. "Mother Mary comes to me, speaking words of wisdom, Let it Be, Let It Be."

A152. During Easter 1960 John and Paul were helping out and working behind the bar at Paul's cousin's pub The Fox and Hounds in Caversham. One night, John and Paul played their only gig as a double act, naming themselves the Nerk Twins. A nerk is a Liverpool slang term for a fool!

A153. 'I Feel Fine' starts with a single, percussive feedback note. During the recording session Paul plucked his bass guitar, and John's guitar, which was leaning against Paul's amplifier, picked up feedback. Producer George Martin decided to add the sound created to the beginning of the record. It is widely believed to be the first use of feedback on a rock record.

A154. Paul has been quoted that his chauffeur coined the phrase. Paul asked him how he was, to which he replied, "Oh, working hard, working eight days a week."

A155. 'Got to Get You Into My Life' has been covered by a number of bands, but arguably none better than Earth, Wind & Fire's innovative version.

A156. 'Lovely Rita' a song on the Sergeant Pepper album, was a meter maid – slang for a traffic warden.

A157. "Here I stand head in hand turn my face to the wall" is the opening to 'You've Got to Hide Your Love Away', which is on the album Help!

A158. He started the Plastic Ono Band with Yoko in 1969.

A159. In November 1974, Elton John released a cover version of 'Lucy in the Sky with Diamonds'. It featured backing vocals and guitar by John Lennon.

A160. 'Ticket To Ride' features in the film Help! with the band goofing around on skis in the Austrian Alps.

Chapter 17

161. What song is featured in the fade-out of 'All You Need is Love'?
     A. From Me To You
     B. Love Me Do
     C. Please Please Me
     D. She Loves You

162. What was the working title to 'Yesterday'?
     A. Boiled Eggs
     B. Fried Eggs
     C. Poached Eggs
     D. Scrambled Eggs

163. Who co-wrote 'Fame' with David Bowie?
     A. John
     B. Paul
     C. George
     D. Ringo

164. How many of the group played on 'Yesterday'?
     A. 1
     B. 2
     C. 3
     D. 4

165. What album did 'Michelle' appear on?
     A. Beatles For Sale
     B. Help!
     C. Revolver
     D. Rubber Soul

166. What was the subject matter of 'Day Tripper'?
    A. Drugs
    B. Holidays
    C. Religion
    D. Young Love

167. How many promotional clips did the band film as part of the 'Intertel Promos'?
    A. 6
    B. 8
    C. 10
    D. 12

168. What instrument does John play in the promotional clips the group made for 'We Can Work It Out'?
    A. Electric Keyboards
    B. Harmonium
    C. Organ
    D. Piano

169. What song starts with "Is there anybody going to listen to my story, all about the girl who came to stay"?
    A. Come Together
    B. Girl
    C. I Saw Her Standing There
    D. Michelle

170. Which of these does Paul play lead guitar on from the 'Revolver' album?
    A. Good Day Sunshine
    B. I'm Only Sleeping
    C. She Said She Said
    D. Taxman

A161. The chorus to 'She Loves You' is featured in the long fade out of 'All You Need is Love'.

A162. Unusually Paul had the complete tune to Yesterday before the lyrics. Whilst working on it, he regularly sang, "Scrambled Eggs, oh you've got such lovely legs" whilst experimenting with the lyrics.

A163. John co-wrote 'Fame' which became Bowie's first US number one. He also provided backing vocals.

A164. Paul was the only member of the group involved with the recording of 'Yesterday'. He played acoustic guitar and was backed by a string quartet of session musicians.

A165. 'Michelle' was on the 'Rubber Soul' album.

A166. The song title 'Day Tripper' is a play on words referring to both a day out and a 'trip' in the sense of a drug experience. In 1970 John described it as a drugs song and in 2004 Paul said it was about LSD.

A167. On 23rd November 1965, the group filmed ten different promotional clips for five songs. These clips were created to save the band having to appear in person on TV shows and also to provide original material to TV shows worldwide. This was an idea way ahead of its time, and an early fore-runner of today's music videos. These promotional clips were called 'Intertel Promos'.

A168. Three promotional clips were made to promote 'We Can Work It Out' and in each of them John was filmed sat at the harmonium.

A169. 'Girl', a popular song on the album 'Rubber Soul', starts with "Is there anybody going to listen to my story, all about the girl who came to stay".

A170. Paul played lead guitar on 'Taxman' on the album 'Revolver'. It includes a stunning guitar solo demonstrating that Paul was an incredibly talented and accomplished musician.

171. How many motion pictures do the Beatles appear in?
    A. 4
    B. 5
    C. 6
    D. 7

172. When was the first of these films released?
    A. 1962
    B. 1964
    C. 1966
    D. 1968

173. When was the last of these films released?
    A. 1968
    B. 1969
    C. 1970
    D. 1971

174. What was the last film they starred in?
    A. A Hard Day's Night
    B. Help!
    C. Let It Be
    D. Yellow Submarine

175. What was Paul's grandfather in 'It's A Hard Day's Night' often referred to as?
    A. Casual
    B. Cheeky
    C. Clean
    D. Crisp

176. Who originally said "It's A Hard Day's Night"?
    A. John
    B. Paul
    C. George
    D. Ringo

177. Who shuffles and deals the playing cards on the train?
    A. John
    B. Paul
    C. George
    D. Ringo

178. Who met his future wife while filming the "It's A Hard Day's Night" movie?
    A. John
    B. Paul
    C. George
    D. Ringo

179. Who is the first Beatle seen in the film Help! ?
    A. John
    B. Paul
    C. George
    D. Ringo

180. What is the name of the leader of the cult religion in the movie "Help!" ?
    A. Clang
    B. Cling
    C. Clong
    D. Clung

A171. The Beatles appeared in five movies.

A172. Their first film was released in 1964.

A173. Their last film was released in 1970.

A174. Their last film was 'Let It Be'.

A175. The grandfather was often referred to as clean. It was almost a catchphrase the word was used so much. It was an ironic joke as the actor who played the part, Wilfred Brambell, was most famous for playing a scruffy smelly rag and bone man in a popular TV show at the time called Steptoe & Son.

A176. Ringo had originally used the phrase as an off-the-cuff remark after the group had been working all night.

A177. Ringo. He was doing a classic Liverpool shuffle (as in not shuffling the cards at all).

A178. George Harrison met his future wife Pattie Boyd during filming of the movie.

A179. Ringo. This first shot of the film is a close-up of his hand, showing a ring that features as the primary plot device of the movie.

A180. The leader of the cult religion is Clang.

181. What is the name of the palace that The Beatles visit in Help! ?
    A. Buckingham Palace
    B. Kensington Palace
    C. Summer Palace
    D. Winter Palace

182. What was the title of the Beatles' third film?
    A. Magical Mystery Tour
    B. Mediaeval Mystery Tour
    C. Methodical Mystery Tour
    D. Mystical Mystery Tour

183. Which is the only George Harrison composition in the film?
    A. Blue Jay Way
    B. Hello, Goodbye
    C. Penny Lane
    D. Your Mother Should Know

184. What is the name of the captain in 'Yellow Submarine'?
    A. Frank
    B. Fraser
    C. Fred
    D. Frodo

185. Which of these songs appear in the movie 'Yellow Submarine'?
    A. All You Need Is Love
    B. Lucy in the Sky with Diamonds
    C. Only a Northern Song
    D. When I'm Sixty Four

186. What is the last song in the movie 'Yellow Submarine'?
    A. All Together Now
    B. Eleanor Rigby
    C. Hey Bulldog
    D. It's All Too Much

187. Where was the impromptu concert at the end of 'Let It Be' performed?
    A. On a building rooftop
    B. On a river boat
    C. On a steam train
    D. On an open top bus tour

188. Which guest musician played organ and piano on 'Let it Be'?
    A. Dave Brubeck
    B. Ray Charles
    C. Billy Preston
    D. Cecil Taylor

189. What Academy Award did 'Let it Be' win?
    A. Best Original Screenplay
    B. Best Original Song Score
    C. Best Picture
    D. Best Sound Editing

190. What is the last song in the movie 'Let it Be'?
    A. Across the Universe
    B. Get Back
    C. Let It Be
    D. The Long and Winding Road

Chapter 19: Answers

A181. Buckingham Palace.

A182. Their third film was called Magical Mystery Tour.

A183. 'Blue Jay Way' was written by George. It is named after a street in the Hollywood Hills where he stayed in 1967.

A184. Fred, and he was often referred to as Old Fred by the band.

A185. It's a trick question as all of these songs were in the movie. Give yourself a bonus point if you knew that.

A186. 'All Together Now' is the final song in the movie.

A187. The finale was filmed on the rooftop of the Apple Studios building in Central London.

A188. Billy Preston was the musician who played in the movie, both in the studio and on the rooftop.

A189. The movie won an Oscar in 1970 for Best Original Sound Score.

A190. 'Get Back' is the last song in the movie, performed during the memorable rooftop sequence.

191. What song has "beep, beep'm beep beep yeah" as the backing vocals?
    A. Back in the U.S.S.R.
    B. Day Tripper
    C. Drive My Car
    D. Magical Mystery Tour

192. What is 'Norwegian Wood' about?
    A. A bird of paradise
    B. A log cabin
    C. An extra-martial affair
    D. Scandinavian food

193. What is 'The Beatles' album title more commonly known as?
    A. The Black Album
    B. The Grey Album
    C. The White Album
    D. The Yellow Album

194. Which song did the group sing on their only live appearance on 'Top of the Pops'?
    A. And I Love Her
    B. Here Comes The Sun
    C. Hey Jude
    D. Paperback Writer

195. Which musician introduced cannabis to the group?
    A. Marty Balin
    B. Bob Dylan
    C. Roger McGuinn
    D. Neil Young

196. Which song includes the lyrics, "Doesn't have a point of view, knows not where he's going to"?
    A. I Am The Walrus
    B. Magical Mystery Tour
    C. Nowhere Man
    D. The Fool On The Hill

197. Which song did John call his "first real major piece of work"?
    A. A Day In the Life
    B. In My Life
    C. Strawberry Fields Forever
    D. The Ballad of John and Yoko

198. Who did Paul write 'Step Inside Love' for?
    A. Cilla Black
    B. Mary Hopkin
    C. Sandie Shaw
    D. Dusty Springfield

199. What did 'The High Priest of LSD' Timothy Leary declare The Beatles to be?
    A. Eccentrics
    B. Freaks
    C. Mutants
    D. Wackos

200. What song used words adapted and embellished from Leary's book 'The Psychedelic Experience'?
    A. Doctor Robert
    B. Got To Get You Into My Life
    C. She Said She Said
    D. Tomorrow Never Knows

Chapter 20: Answers

A191. 'Drive My Car' features the backing vocals "beep beep'm beep beep yeah."

A192. 'Norwegian Wood' is about an extra-marital affair.

A193. 'The Beatles' album, released in 1968, had a plain white cover, and quickly became known as 'The White Album'.

A194. The group's only live appearance on Top of the Pops was on 16th June 1966 to promote 'Paperback Writer'.

A195. On 28th August 1964 Bob Dylan introduced the group to cannabis in their suite at the Delmonico Hotel in New York City. Whilst the group stayed there, over 200,000 incoming calls were received by the hotel switchboard.

A196. 'Nowhere Man' includes the lyrics "Doesn't have a point of view, knows not where he's going to. Isn't he a bit like ma and you."

A197. John called 'In My Life' his "first real major piece of work".

A198. 'Step Inside Love' was one of a number of songs Paul and/or John wrote for their close friend and fellow Liverpudlian Cilla Black.

A199. Leary was quoted as saying, "I declare that The Beatles are mutants. Prototypes of evolutionary agents sent by God, endowed with a mysterious power to create a new human species."

A200. A number of words to 'Tomorrow Never Knows' were borrowed, adapted and embellished from Leary's book 'The Psychedelic Experience'. When writing the song, John drew inspiration from his experiences with LSD and from Leary's book.

201. What was the first single released after the death of Brian Epstein?
    A. Get Back
    B. Hello Goodbye
    C. Lady Madonna
    D. The Long And Winding Road

202. Who is selling poppies from a tray in 'Penny Lane'?
    A. A banker
    B. A barber
    C. A nurse
    D. A fireman

203. What was released as a double-A side to 'Penny Lane'?
    A. Eleanor Rigby
    B. Getting Better
    C. Strawberry Fields Forever
    D. With A Little Help From My Friends

204. What did John regard as his finest work with The Beatles?
    A. A Day In the Life
    B. In My Life
    C. Strawberry Fields Forever
    D. The Ballad of John and Yoko

205. What song did Ringo sing from the Sergeant Pepper album?
    A. Lovely Rita
    B. She's Leaving Home
    C. When I'm Sixty Four
    D. With A Little Help From My Friends

206. What colour are the trees in 'Lucy in the Sky With Diamonds'?
    A. Apricot
    B. Peach
    C. Papaya
    D. Tangerine

207. How many albums does 'Eleanor Rigby' appear on?
    A. 2
    B. 3
    C. 4
    D. 5

208. How many holes are there in Blackburn, Lancashire as per the lyrics of 'A Day In The Life'?
    A. Two thousand
    B. Three thousand
    C. Four thousand
    D. Five thousand

209. What musical instrument provides the ending to 'A Day In The Life'?
    A. Double Bass
    B. Piano
    C. Trumpet
    D. Viola

210. Who are the grandchildren named in 'When I'm Sixty-Four'?
    A. Valerie, Chad and Damon
    B. Vera, Chuck and Dave
    C. Victoria, Chip and Dan
    D. Vivien, Chas and Daryl

Chapter 21: Answers

I hope you're having fun, and getting most of the answers right.

A201. 'Hello Goodbye' was the first single released after the death of Epstein.

A202. The lyrics to 'Penny Lane' include, "Behind the shelter in the middle of the roundabout, the pretty nurse is selling poppies from a tray."

A203.'Strawberry Fields Forever' was released as a double-A side with 'Penny Lane'.

A204. John regarded 'Strawberry Fields Forever' as his finest work with the group.

A205. Ringo sang lead vocal on 'With a Little Help From My Friends'. The first line to the sog was originally written as "What would you think if I sang out of tune? Would you throw ripe tomatoes at me?" That was changed as the song writing evolved to "What would you think if I sang out of tune? Would you stand up and walk out on me?" A subsequent recording of the song in 1968 by Joe Cocker became a hit single and an anthem for the hippy era.

A206. 'Lucy in the Sky With Diamonds' starts with the dreamy lyrics, "Picture yourself in a boat on a river, with tangerine trees and marmalade skies."

A207. 'Eleanor Rigby' is on five albums. They are Revolver; Anthology 2; Yellow Submarine Songtrack; Love and 1.

A208. "I read the news today, oh boy; Four thousand holes in Blackburn, Lancashire; And though the holes were rather small; They had to count them all."

A209. A crashing piano chord provides the ending to 'A Day in the Life'. It was created by three pianos simultaneously playing an E major chord.

A210. 'When I'm Sixty-Four' includes the line, "Grandchildren on your knee, Vera, Chuck and Dave."

211. What song starts with the introduction to the French National Anthem 'La Marseillaise'?
    A. A Day In The Life
    B. All You Need Is Love
    C. Revolution
    D. Sergeant Pepper's Lonely Hearts Club Band

212. What is the name of the priest in 'Eleanor Rigby'?
    A. Father McCarthy
    B. Father McCartney
    C. Father McIntyre
    D. Father McKenzie

213. What was the last song the group performed live in front of a paying audience?
    A. Day Tripper
    B. Johnny B Goode
    C. Long Tall Sally
    D. Twist and Shout

214. Which song includes the line "oompah, oompah, stick it up your jumper"?
    A. A Day In The Life
    B. I Am The Walrus
    C. Ob-La-Di Ob-La-Da
    D. Sergeant Pepper's Lonely Hearts Club Band

215. Who sketched the idea for the 'Abbey Road' album cover?
    A. John
    B. Paul
    C. George
    D. Ringo

216. Which film was 'A Fool On The Hill' featured in?
   A. A Hard Days Night
   B. Help!
   C. Magical Mystery Tour
   D. Yellow Submarine

217. Who played tenor saxophone on the studio recording of 'Lady Madonna'?
   A. Stan Getz
   B. Harry Klein
   C. David Sanborn
   D. Ronnie Scott

218. What was the name of the compilation album released in 2000?
   A. 1
   B. Exclusively 1
   C. Number One Hits
   D. Only Number 1s

219. Which album, released in 1969, included the songs 'Here Comes The Sun' and 'Something'?
   A. Abbey Road
   B. Let It Be
   C. The White Album
   D. Yellow Submarine

220. What is The Beatles' best-selling album of all time?
   A. Abbey Road
   B. Revolver
   C. Rubber Soul
   D. Sergeant Pepper's Lonely Hearts Club Band

Chapter 22: Answers

A211. 'All You Need Is Love' starts with the introduction to 'La Marseilleaise' and the song also contains parts of other musical works, including 'In The Mood' by Glenn Miller.

A212. Father McKenzie is the priest in 'Eleanor Rigby'. Originally Paul had written Father McCartney but he changed it so as to avoid any confusion with his own name.

A213. 'Long Tall Sally' was the last song the Beatles performed live in front of a paying audience. It was a fitting song to finish with, as it had been a staple of their live performances since the days of The Quarrymen.

A214. "oompah, oompah, stick it up your jumper" is one of the many esoteric lines from 'I Am The Walrus'.

A215. Paul had sketched his ideas as to what he would like for the album cover and freelance photographer Iain Macmillan took the iconic picture. If you are interested in this kind of thing, he used a Hasselblad camera with a 500mm wide angle lens, f22 aperture and a shutter speed of 1/500 seconds.

A216. 'A Fool On The Hill' was in the 'Magical Mystery Tour' movie. The segment in the movie that showed Paul fooling about on a hill was filmed in the South of France.

A217. Ronnie Scott is credited with playing tenor saxophone on the studio recording of 'Lady Madonna' whilst Harry Klein played baritone saxophone.

A218. The compilation album was called '1'. It includes the 27 Beatles songs that went to number one in the United Kingdom on the Record Retailer Top 50 chart or in the United States on the Billboard Hot 100 chart. The songs were digitally remastered for the album by George Martin and the album reached number 1 in 35 countries.

A219. The group's last-recorded album 'Abbey Road' included the hit singles 'Here Comes The Sun' and 'Something'. Incidentally 'Somtething' is the only Harrison composition to appear as a Beatles A-side.

A220. Album sales are notoriously hard to measure, and there is a certain fudge factor especially for older albums that weren't counted correctly. That said, it is generally accepted that 'Sergeant Pepper's Lonely Hearts Club Band' is the groups' best-selling album of all time, with an estimated 32 million album sales worldwide.

Chapter 23

221. Which of these is not a Beatles album?
   A. Beatles For Sale
   B. Meet The Beatles
   C. The Beatles
   D. With The Beatles

222. What was the first single released on the Apple Records label?
   A. Back in the USSR
   B. Get Back
   C. Hey Jude
   D. Ob-La-Di, Ob-La-Da

223. What was the first Beatles album released on the Apple Records label?
   A. Abbey Road
   B. Hey Jude
   C. The Beatles
   D. Yellow Submarine

224. Which song made reference to Chairman Mao Zedong?
   A. Back in the USSR
   B. Get Back
   C. Let It Be
   D. Revolution

225. Who was 'Hey Jude' written about?
   A. Julian Clary
   B. Julian Fellowes
   C. Julian Lennon
   D. Julian Sands

226. What 1977 demo song by John was completed by the other three Beatles in 1994?
   A. And Your Bird Can Sing
   B. Blackbird
   C. Flying
   D. Free As A Bird

227. How many Grammy awards have The Beatles won?
   A. 5
   B. 7
   C. 9
   D. 11

228. What was the name of the trilogy of albums released in the 1990s featuring demos, studio out-takes and miscellaneous recordings?
   A. Anthology
   B. Escapology
   C. Methodology
   D. Musicology

229. Where are the girls who "really knock me out" from on 'Back in the USSR'?
   A. Belarus
   B. Georgia
   C. Moscow
   D. Ukraine

230. Who played lead guitar on 'While My Guitar Gently Weeps'?
   A. Jeff Beck
   B. Eric Clapton
   C. Jimmy Page
   D. Keith Richards

A221. 'Meet The Beatles' is the odd one out.

A222. 'Hey Jude' was the first single released on the Apple Records label, being released on 26th August 1968 in the US and 30th August 1968 in the UK.

A223. 'The Beatles' was the first Beatles album released on the Apple Records label, being released in November 1968.

A224. 'Revolution' contains the line, "But if you go carrying pictures of Chairman Mao; You ain't gone make it with anyone anyhow."

A225. 'Hey Jude' was written by Paul about Julian Lennon. He wrote it to comfort Julian, after his father John had left his wife Cynthia for Yoko Ono. The lyrics champion a positive outlook on a sad situation.

A226. Based on a 1977 demo recorded by John in New York City, 'Free As A Bird' was completed by the other three Beatles seventeen years later and released as the lead single from the 'Anthology' project.

A227. According to the official grammy.com website, The Beatles won a total of just 7 Grammy awards, and only 4 while they were together.

A228. Anthology 1, 2 and 3 were compilation albums that featured demos, studio out-takes and miscellaneous recordings. They formed part of 'The Anthology Project' which also included a book and a TV documentary series.

A229. The lyrics to 'Back in the USSR' include, "The Ukraine girls really knock me out, they leave the West behind".

A230. 'While My Guitar Gently Weeps' features a guest appearance of Eric Clapton on lead guitar. Clapton's solo was treated with automatic double tracking, a technique used to enhance the guitar's sound during the mixing process. After the recording, Clapton gave George his solid red Gibson Les Paul guitar he used during the recording session, which George later named "Lucy" after redhead comedienne Lucille Ball. The guitar was stolen in a burglary from Harrison's home in Beverly Hills in 1973, and was recovered some months later. George then kept "Lucy" with him for the rest of his life. It is one of the most famous electric guitars in the world and is priceless.

Chapter 24

231. Who did the band record 'Get Back' and Don't Let Me
   Down' with?
   A. Joe Cocker
   B. Billy Preston
   C. Bill Withers
   D. Bobby Womack

232. Who is the only Beatle to have published an
   autobiography?
   A. John
   B. Paul
   C. George
   D. Ringo

233. Who was Liverpool Airport renamed after?
   A. John
   B. Paul
   C. George
   D. Ringo

234. Which of the following songs was not banned by the BBC?
   A. A Day In The Life
   B. I Am The Walrus
   C. Lucy In The Sky With Diamonds
   D. With A Little Help From My Friends

235. Which album had all of its songs written by John and
   Paul?
   A. A Hard Day's Night
   B. Help!
   C. Please Please Me
   D. With The Beatles

236. How many times is 'nah' sung on 'Hey Jude'?
    A. 210
    B. 220
    C. 230
    D. 240

237. Who played left handed?
    A. John
    B. Paul
    C. George
    D. Ringo

238. Where did John get the inspiration for 'Good Morning, Good Morning'?
    A. A TV commercial for Corn Flakes
    B. Monty Python's Flying Circus
    C. Peyton Place
    D. The Avengers

239. How many UK number one singles did the group have?
    A. 13
    B. 15
    C. 17
    D. 19

240. Which is the only day of the week not mentioned in 'Lady Madonna'?
    A. Monday
    B. Wednesday
    C. Saturday
    D. Sunday

A231. The band recorded the songs with Billy Preston. The single releases were credited to "the Beatles with Billy Preston". He is the only non-member of the band to receive a performance credit on a record.

A232. George is the only Beatle who has published an autobiography. "I, Me, Mine" is a rather odd autobiography with the minority of the book being what could be termed as autobiographical and the majority being song lyrics, photos and drawings. It was originally printed as a limited edition of just 2,000 copies and as such it is a collector's item.

A233. Liverpool Airport was renamed Liverpool John Lennon Airport in 2001.

A234. 'With A Little Help From My Friends' was the only song not banned by the BBC. The others were deemed to reference drugs or sex, as in "you've let your knickers down" in 'I Am The Walrus'.

A235. The album 'A Hard Day's Night' had all its songs written by John and Paul.

A236. 'Nah' as in "nah, nah nah nah-nah-nah nah, nah-nah-nah nah, Hey Jude", the coda which fills the second half of the record, occurs an incredible 240 times!

A237. Paul plays his guitar left handed, but he does most other things, including writing, with his right hand.

A238. John got the inspiration for 'Good Morning, Good Morning' from a TV commercial for Corn Flakes. The words to the commercial were, "Good morning, good morning, The best to you each morning, Sunshine breakfast, Kellogg's Corn Flakes, Crisp and full of sun."

A239. The group had seventeen number one singles on the UK charts.

A240. Saturday is the only day of the week not mentioned in 'Lady Madonna'.

241. Where did the group film the promotional film for 'Strawberry Fields Forever'?
    A. Hyde Park
    B. Knole Park
    C. Stoke Park
    D. Sutton Park

242. Which album was Phil Spector credited as producer?
    A. Abbey Road
    B. Beatles For Sale
    C. Let It Be
    D. Magical Mystery Tour

243. How long is the book in 'Paperback Writer'?
    A. 500 pages
    B. 750 pages
    C. 1,000 pages
    D. 2,000 pages

244. Where did Paul come up with 'The Long and Winding Road'?
    A. England
    B. Ireland
    C. Scotland
    D. Wales

245. Who crossed Abbey Road first?
    A. John
    B. Paul
    C. George
    D. Ringo

246. What song was the group's last number one single?
   A. Get Back
   B. Hey Jude
   C. The Ballad Of John And Yoko
   D. The Long And Winding Road

247. Which song did Frank Sinatra call the "greatest love song ever written"?
   A. And I Love Her
   B. Something
   C. Yesterday
   D. You're Going To Lose That Girl

248. Which song did the group sing on their final ever live TV appearance?
   A. Across The Universe
   B. All You Need Is Love
   C. Hey Jude
   D. The Ballad of John and Yoko

249. When were The Beatles inducted into the Rock and Roll Hall of Fame?
   A. 1982
   B. 1984
   C. 1986
   D. 1988

250. Who said, "I hope we passed the audition" at the end of the movie 'Let It Be'?
   A. John
   B. Paul
   C. George
   D. Ringo

Chapter 25: Answers

Here are the answers to the final set of questions.

A241. The promotional film for 'Strawberry Fields Forever' was filmed at Knole Park in Kent.

A242. The tapes to 'Let It Be' were on the shelf because there was a lot of animosity between the group members at the time. So John scooped up the tapes and - without the others' permission - gave them to Phil Spector to finish. He gave the songs his 'wall of sound' treatment and was credited as the producer of the record. Paul voiced his displeasure at the way Spector had not captured the intended strip-down aesthetic of a number of the songs on the album and he later was behind the 2003 release of Let It Be... Naked which presented some tracks without most of Spector's embellishments.

A243. "It's a thousand pages, give or take a few."

A244. The title 'The Long and Winding Road' was inspired by Paul's sight of a road "stretching up into the hills" in the remote Scottish Highlands.

A245. John is first then Ringo, then Paul, then George. John, Ringo and Paul all wore suits by Savile Row tailor Tommy Nutter. George wore denim.

A246. The group's last number one single in the UK was 'The Ballad of John and Yoko' and the last number one in the US was 'The Long and Winding Road'. Give yourself a bonus point if you knew that.

A247. Sinatra declared 'Something' to be the "greatest love song ever written". Written by George, the song is generally considered to be about Pattie Boyd, his first wife.

A248. On 25th June 1967 the group made their final live TV appearance as a group when they closed the 'Our World' show, the first live international satellite TV program with an estimated audience of 500-700 million people, with a stunning memorable performance of 'All You Need Is Love'. The group invited a number of their friends including Eric Clapton, Marianne Faithfull, Mick Jagger and Keith Moon to help create a happy vibe and join in the song's chorus.

A249. Mick Jagger inducted The Beatles into the Rock and Roll Hall of Fame in 1988.

A250. John said, "I hope we passed the audition" at the end of the movie 'Let It Be'.

That's it. I hope you enjoyed this book, and I hope you got most of the answers right. I also hope you learnt a few new things about The Beatles.

I would like to acknowledge the BeatlesBible.com website which has been invaluable during my research for this book.

If you saw anything wrong, or if you have any comments, please get in touch via the glowwormpress.com website. I do read all message sent in, and this book has already been updated as a result of messages left by others.

Thanks for reading, and if you did enjoy the book, please leave a positive review on Amazon.

Printed in Great Britain
by Amazon

11583980R00061